ONCE UPON A RHYME

IMAGINATION FOR A NEW GENERATION

West London

Edited by Sarah Marshall

Young Writers

First published in Great Britain in 2004 by:
Young Writers
Remus House
Coltsfoot Drive
Peterborough
PE2 9JX
Telephone: 01733 890066
Website: www.youngwriters.co.uk

SB ISBN 1 84460 483 7

Foreword

Young Writers was established in 1991 and has been passionately devoted to the promotion of reading and writing in children and young adults ever since. The quest continues today. Young Writers remains as committed to engendering the fostering of burgeoning poetic and literary talent as ever.

This year's Young Writers competition has proven as vibrant and dynamic as ever and we are delighted to present a showcase of the best poetry from across the UK. Each poem has been carefully selected from a wealth of *Once Upon A Rhyme* entries before ultimately being published in this, our twelfth primary school poetry series.

Once again, we have been supremely impressed by the overall high quality of the entries we have received. The imagination, energy and creativity which has gone into each young writer's entry made choosing the best poems a challenging and often difficult but ultimately hugely rewarding task - the general high standard of the work submitted amply vindicating this opportunity to bring their poetry to a larger appreciative audience.

We sincerely hope you are pleased with our final selection and that you will enjoy *Once Upon A Rhyme West London* for many years to come.

Contents

St Mary Abbots CE Primary School

St Mary's School, Hammersmith

St Peter's CE Primary School, Hammersmith

Rishi Anand (8)   180
Oliver Swan (8)   181

The Fox Primary School
Molly McMorrow (9)   182
Elisha Jelen (10)   183
Edie Gill Holder (10)   184
Ruby Lott-Lavigna (10)   185
Mo Langmuir (9)   186
Tatiana Zoe Barnes (9)   187

West Acton Primary School
Lauren Fisher (9)   188
Kayli Homer (10)   189
Ethan Harry Hart-Badger (9)   190
Ameenah Aumeed (9)   191
Amanda Lee (10)   192
Hannah Roiter (10)   193
Mona Roozfarakh (9)   194
Laura Alicia Hall-Williams (9)   195

The Poems

Hope And Happiness

Is there hope for harmony in this world?
Will there be happiness for needy people?
Can poor people look forward to a better life?
Will hope bring families together?

Can people trust each other?
Will we ever live in happiness and not fear?
Can we care about someone else besides ourselves?
Will we ever learn to love, then to learn about hatred?

Is it possible for children to learn that we are all one?
Do we always have to hate someone just because of how they look?
Can we live together without being afraid?
Is it possible for children to love and not hate?

Evan Mamand (11)
Berrymede Junior School

The Great Phoenix

It is so strong, yet so beautiful,
It has so many pretty colours,
Dashing, diving, darting and . . .
Suddenly, it turns into a furious
Ferocious, red-hot, flaming,
Flying beast.
He has bright yellow, glowing eyes
Like the colour of the sun.
What am I?

Terry Benham (11)
Berrymede Junior School

Faith

Why are so many people dying?
Why are there so many people crying?
Why can't the world just live in peace?
Why can't there be a day without police?

Chorus

People, learn to love one another,
People rejoice with their father and mother,
People show their good side
Because it's your faith that you can't hide.

Why are the skies all turning grey?
Why can't we love without delay?
Why is there so much war?
Why are we hating so much more?

Chorus

Why can't world leaders set an example?
Why can't they give children a good sample?
Why is the world turning greedy?
Why not think of people who are needy?

Chorus

Manal Manzoor (11)
Berrymede Junior School

Hallowe'en

People had pumpkins with candles inside,
It was scary,
People dress up in scary costumes,
Then something touched me,
I got scared,
I started to run getting faster and faster,
My mind went all blurry,
I couldn't see straight,
Then . . .

I turned around and I saw,
Lots of children ringing the doorbells,
I thought they were coming after me,
Then . . .

Boo!

Someone jumped at me,
I fell,
I got shaky.

Laura Tullio (10)
Berrymede Junior School

Anger

Anger is like a blaze of fire
Going through your head.
You walk around punching stuff
Just wanting to kill.

Zainab Gbolahan (10)
Berrymede Junior School

Who?

Who told the grass to be green,
And told the wind not to be seen?

Who taught the birds to build a nest,
And told the trees to take a rest?

Who made the woods full of trees,
And said that honey was made by bees?

Who told the rivers to flow each way,
And told the weather to change each day?

Or when the stars decide to blow out,
Who lights them up again without a doubt?

Now why do you suppose,
That no one tells me if they know?

Answer: Nature.

Beatrice Aboagye-Williams (10)
Berrymede Junior School

Think Of Africa

Think of Africa . . . think of Africa,
They are in need of aid.
'Will you help . . . ?'
'Are you going to?'

Lots of drought in North Africa,
People suffer in Somalia.
There isn't that much food,
Lots of racism calling in South Africa.

Chorus

Help . . . help them.
Help . . . help them.
Don't forget about Africa.
Don't forget about Africa.

Somalia, Ethiopia and many other countries are in danger,
Make them feel . . . *happy,* not . . . *sad!*
They need your . . . *heellp!*

Chorus

Help them . . . help them.
Help them . . . help them.
Don't forget about Africa.
Don't forget about Africa.

AbdulQadir Yusuf (10)
Berrymede Junior School

The Wise Dragon

His mum calls him Fiery
Because he burns everything.
His table manners are very rude
Because he bangs his knife and fork.
He is not kind to his little brother
Because he whacks him with his wings.
He sprints through the air when he flies,
Sometimes he gets cross and growls
Because his little brother annoys him.
He likes to eat people
Because they are meat.
He sleeps in the morning
Because he is nocturnal.
But most of all he is wise
Because he always listen to his mum.

Joel Carne (6)
Berrymede Junior School

The Swirly River

I hear a river rushing
Through the fields and marshes.
It came from the mountains,
Heading to the sea.

The river curls gently
Like a piece of spaghetti.
It hisses as it moves
Like an angry snake.

The rustling river ripples,
Making shapes in the water.
The river splashes down its path,
Sprinting from the mountains.

At last it sees the end of its path,
It sees fish and open water,
Now it is feeling tired and sleepy,
Home!

Jerrick Carne (7)
Berrymede Junior School

Christmas

Christmas to me is having fun,
Hitting people with snowballs on the run.
Receiving gifts and dying to open them
While they're next to the tree.
At Christmas we then open our presents and see.
Standing there is a snowman,
Then I come out to play in the snow.
Making myself and my family.
Watching the high street lights glow
And eating roast chicken, umm . . . yum-yum,
So then I say bye to Christmas, 'Oh . . . what a bum.'

Angela Marina Fernandes Lobo (11)
Berrymede Junior School

Moon

Shining bright at night,
All alone hanging like a string,
Waiting for men in big suits,
Waiting for men who are dying to see him,
No man comes . . .
Then . . . he gives up,
He waits for 300 years,
And finally he sees a speck of light
Coming towards him,
Then it gets closer and closer,
Until finally he has man on him,
Will he have man on him again?

Natasha Lamptey (11)
Berrymede Junior School

Christmas

C hildren playing in the snow,
H appy times when family meet,
R eceiving presents, astonished faces,
I nside having a hot Christmas dinner.
S now everywhere,
T ime to have food, tummies rumble.
M agical times when family meet,
A mazed faces when you see all your family,
S itting down in front of the fireplace all warm.

Danielle Purkis (11)
Berrymede Junior School

The Naked Flame

I am candle that needs a friend,
Half of my body has gone which will never mend.
Nobody cares about me at all,
Soon I'm going to have a massive fall.
The only friend I have is fire,
The one I desire.
I have no heartbeat,
Not even a wax sheet.
Why were you pretending to be my friend fire?
I hate you big fat liar.
My body is shrinking,
With the fire drinking.
Why doesn't anyone like me?
Just like the wind destroying the tree.
I feel all alone,
As I am leaving my throne.
I am going fast,
Going,
Going,
Gone.
I am dead at last.

Latika Rana (11)
Berrymede Junior School

The Found Pound

I was on my way to school
When I tripped and looked like a fool.
As I turned around
I found a pound.
So I spent it on sweets
To rot my teeth.

Then one fell out,
'Oh no,' I began to shout.
As we come to the end,
This is the poem I'm going to send.

Joshua Williams (10)
Berrymede Junior School

Windows

There are windows
Looking like a shiny star,
I feel happy.
Crystal pictures
Shining from outside,
A shining star.
I feel quiet and still
Like the sun is falling on me,
Like God is with me.

Alexandra Dardart (7)
Christ Church CE Junior School

The Window

The window reminds me
Of my grandma because she died
And Jesus died on the cross too.
His cloak is very dark red around him,
Stars are in the Earth, twinkling in the world
And I bet one star is my grandma, twinkling in the sky.

Natasha Matthews (7)
Christ Church CE Junior School

Fireworks

Fireworks are going,
Fireworks are glowing,
They smell like fire,
Taste like a flower,
Bright like the god,
Eyes like an eagle,
Wonderful like the wind,
Beautiful like an angel,
Looks like an exploding fire
And bright like the sun.

James Cozier-Alexander (8)
Christ Church CE Junior School

Peace

What is peace?
Is it when war will cease?
Is it when we beat the opponent
And hold up fighting for the moment?
Is it when slavery is abolished and gone
Or when the light of God is needly shone?
Is it when the apocalypse never comes
And the four horsemen get burnt in the sun?
Is it when hate is no longer a word
Or when we can sing to nature and bird?
Is it when the planet's absolutely together
Just like a shoe made of tightly bound leather?

What is *peace*?

James Fell (10)
Flora Gardens School

A Kind Child

My mother says she is proud of me
And happy she will be.
She says I have a kind heart in every little way.
I'm kind to my brothers and sister,
To the poor and servants too.
I try to help the people who are sick.
I try to help my mother and father.
I also try to help them altogether.
So my mother says she's so lucky 'cause she got me.

Mary Elizabeth Hael (11)
Flora Gardens School

Night

Swaying in the breeze,
The grass looked almost alive.

The night was so profoundly silent
That it was almost heavy.

Up in the inky black sky
A massive moon stared back,
Clear and impenetrable.

Then a sharp, clear sound aroused the
                        sleepy darkness
And an owl, perched motionless on a high
                        up branch swooped down.

Natalie Pearson (11)
Flora Gardens School

Chairlift Ride

Waiting in an endless queue,
Excited, but irritated too.

When will our turn come?
Haven't got a clue.

Before we know it,
We're there at the gate.

Standing ready,
Here it comes, really fast.

Sitting in the chairlift,
Floating in the air.

What a beautiful sight,
The countryside seems.

Time to get off,
And join the other queue.

Which will lead us to
The world we had just left.

But the fun isn't over yet
We have to go back down . . .

Tumbling down . . .

Abida Rahimi (11)
Flora Gardens School

Stars At Night

Shiny stars in the night so clear
And bright yellow or white
Glittering in the dark,
Stays with the moon
Loads of stars around me.

Looking, shape and size
Wonderful or beautiful
All stars are amazing
Imagining they're here,
I have a star that plays
With me at the chocolate bar.

The sky is dark and I see sparks
Shiny as silver
Great to look at and beg for
More shiny stars around me.

My star and I play
Together as a couple
We play and have fun,
I dream that there are
Loads of stars around me
Who want to play.

Zainab Butt (10)
Flora Gardens School

The Magic Box
(Based on 'Magic Box' by Kit Wright)

I will put in the box . . .
An invincible knight in shining armour,
The most humid rainforest in the world,
All the colourful fish in the bluest pond.

I will put in the box . . .
The greenest berry imaginable to mankind,
The biggest wave of the stormy ocean,
The brightest spark in the darkest part of the world.

My box is made from rubies, ice, gold and sapphires,
My box smells like smelly socks,
The lid is a dinosaur's head,
It feels like sponge.

I shall dive in the box,
In the bluest sea in the world,
Then swim with the fishes and dolphins,
And wash ashore on the hottest beach.

Connor Richardson   (7)
Manor House School

The Magic Box

(Based on 'Magic Box' by Kit Wright)

I will put in the box . . .
The brightest colour in the universe,
The darkest enchanted forest in the world,
And the most fascinating Atlantic Ocean.

I will put in the box . . .
The biggest factory in Italy,
The farthest country in the world,
And an incredible, poisonous snake.

I will put in the box . . .
The greatest shark in India,
The sweetest, greenest berry,
And the roughest waves in Canada.

I will put in the box . . .
The most vicious tiger in England,
The nearest island of New Zealand,
And the extreme Fantasy Park.

My box has dog claws as hinges,
It has leaves, sticks and rulers for a lid,
And plates for a box,
It has chocolates for secrets like caramel and Snickers.

I shall fly in my box
Over the highest hill of Mount Everest,
To the Black Sea in Dubai,
And swoop like a seagull at the beach.

Sachran Gill (7)
Manor House School

The Magic Box

(Based on 'Magic Box' by Kit Wright)

I will put in the box . . .
The deepest part of the Atlantic Ocean,
The most bloodthirsty and rarest starfish of the
Darkest and dampest swamp,
And the brightest and most amazing star in the universe.

I will put in the box . . .
The biggest and dampest rock in the Amazon rainforest,
A dusty, old pirate boat sailing the Indian Ocean,
The most beautiful deer in the brightest forest.

I will put in the box . . .
The rarest animal called a Tankaman,
The largest dragon from China,
And a humid cloud that sways from side to side.

I will put in the box . . .
The feather of an eagle,
A swish of web from the biggest spider in the oldest garage,
A slice of King Henry VIII's beard.

My box is made from tiger skin,
And dinosaur scales with sabre-tooth fangs,
Its hinges are the claws of a wolf.

I shall float in my box
Over the salty waters of the Red Sea,
Resting on a giant bed
And relaxing in the breeze.

Manraj Sidhu (8)
Manor House School

The Magic Box

(Based on 'Magic Box' by Kit Wright)

I will put in the box . . .
A twisted wave on a dark, stormy night,
The leaves of the biggest willow tree,
The sweetest blueberry known to mankind.

I will put in the box . . .
A glistening photograph I will remember forever,
The fizziest cola from the stream of the River Nile,
And the dampest forest of all of Abasoz.

I will put in the box . . .
The slowest working river in Perth, Australia,
The biggest cloud swishing in the breeze,
And the spikiest chair, which could kill with one touch.

I will put in the box . . .
A splash of the whitest cream ever,
The smell of the slimiest perfume,
And the loudest stereo that a frog dances to.

My box was my great, great, great, great grandfather's box,
It is fashioned from unicorn's skin,
And it smells like roses,
From a gardener's garden.

I shall sliver in my box,
On the top of a dragon's tooth,
Which came from Siberia,
And over the Chinese River.

Madeleine Witney (9)
Manor House School

The Magic Box

(Based on 'Magic Box' by Kit Wright)

I will put in the box . . .
A glowing light from the South Pole,
A glittering star in the bright sky,
And a glistening red, cool car.

I will put in the box . . .
Fizzy lemon juice from the colourful sea,
The saltiest water in the bluest ocean,
And green Coke from North America.

My box is silver and gold,
It's made from sparkling lights,
The lid is fashioned from Smarties
And crunchy biscuits.

I shall dance in the box,
In a very big hall that has a beautiful garden,
And I will dance,
On the hard wooden floor.

Kareena Dhother (7)
Manor House School

The Magic Box

(Based on 'Magic Box' by Kit Wright)

I will put in the box . . .
The most twisted and juicy berry of all,
A bloodsucking vampire eating a donkey,
An eight-legged freak, ten times the size of us.

I will put in the box . . .
A wizard with magic fizzy Fanta,
The most glowing creature in the universe,
And lots of potions which do magical things.

My box is brand new, it's made out of shark skin,
It's got Chinese dragons on it,
And it has got sparkling fireworks which bring out electric fish,
The fireworks are old.

I shall swim in the box,
In the bluest sea in the universe,
And I shall wash ashore on the beach,
That leads to the Indian Ocean.

Lawrence Jokun-Fearon (8)
Manor House School

The Magic Box

(Based on 'Magic Box' by Kit Wright)

I will put in the box . . .
The softest cloud from the golden heavens,
The hard wind blowing the trees to and fro,
The tallest grass leading to the farmer's crops.

I will put in the box . . .
A big whale swimming in the heavens' cloud,
The biggest wolf howling in the moonlight,
A single bird in the sky chirping alone.

I will put in the box . . .
A grasshopper in a jar trying to get out,
A dancer twirling and twirling until she gets dizzy,
The sound of a carpenter chopping his wood.

I will put in the box . . .
The frost of the North Pole,
A piece of metal from the Eiffel Tower,
A song from an African tribe.

My box is designed from nature,
Little touches of leaves and sticks,
The hinges are carved
From the bark of trees.

I shall feast in my box
On a succulent pig covered in chocolate,
While the cook starts to burn a wig,
Over the big hot pot.

Holly Rollins (8)
Manor House School

The Magic Box

(Based on 'Magic Box' by Kit Wright)

I will put in my box . . .
The whitest snow from Mount Everest,
The darkest night in October,
The strike of midnight.

I will put in the box . . .
The coolest breeze from the South Pole,
The biggest sneeze from the Queen of Scots,
The most colourful rainbow you can see for miles.

I will put in the box,
The shiny slate stolen from a church roof,
The wettest leaf from a sycamore tree,
The most beautiful flower picked from a garden.

I will put in the box . . .
Six, solid, gold, silver and bronze rings,
A sip of the River Nile,
The gloomy ocean from Africa.

The lid of my box is made from a skinned
Rabbit freshly caught on a hunter's moon,
Its hinges are made from flashes of lightning,
The corners are made from a porcupine's skin,
And its sides are made from lemon grass.

I shall fly in my box,
Over the Sydney Harbour,
Seeing the sights of Australia
And touching the Ayers Rock.

Tyran-Zach Meisuria (8)
Manor House School

My Magic Box

(Based on 'Magic Box' by Kit Wright)

I will put in my magic box . . .
The whitest butterfly from Africa,
The most beautiful tulip from Holland,
The best roller coaster from Florida.

I will put in my magic box . . .
The most beautiful seashell from the sea,
The smallest fish from Egypt,
The most beautiful ice crystal from Antarctica.

I will put in my magic box . . .
The deepest gold mine from Russia,
The best picture from New Zealand,
The most active koala from Australia.

My box is made of the finest crystal from India,
With a gold bottom,
The lock is made of the thinnest gold you can get,
With a half-gold, half-crystal key,
Guarded by an alarm which breathes dragon fire
At whoever touches it without the key.

I shall go on the best roller coaster in my box,
And visit every theme park in the world,
Visiting every ride even if it is good or bad too!

Moneet Gill (9)
Manor House School

Gold

Gold is the colour of the shining sun
Gold is the colour of a golden gun
Gold is the colour of a brand new ring
Gold is the royal robe of a king
Gold is the colour of shining sand
Gold is the colour of a big, brass band!

Ciarán van der Westhuizen (9)
Manor House School

Limerick

There is an old man called Fred
Who lives in my garden shed
He comes out at night
And he gives us a fright
Because he looks like he is dead!

Sonia Kharaud (9)
Manor House School

Red

Red is the colour of a red rose burning
Of a Ferrari's wheel turning.

Red is the colour of big, red rocks
Of a ladybird with big spots.

Red is the colour of danger
Of furious anger.

Red is the colour of a flag on a castle
Of a red, red marble.

Red is the colour of a red pen
Of a big red hen.

Red is the colour of a poisoned apple
Of a pot on the table.

Lise Rigaux (9)
Manor House School

The Scary Box

(Based on 'Magic Box' by Kit Wright)

I will put in my box . . .
A piece of a dragon's tail from the fire top mountain,
Some pieces of skin of a Chinese tiger,
A black, dark hole,
Feathers of a burning fire bird.

I will put in my box . . .
A ring from the Atlantic Ocean,
Four big rocks from the Brazilian rainforest,
A 1000-year-old donut,
Ten stars from the galaxy,
Lava from the biggest mountain in the world,
The longest shark in the whole world.

My box is made out of ice,
Jellyfish's jelly
And some spikes.

I will open my box if anybody gets in my way.

Chris Coombes (9)
Manor House School

The Magic Box

(Based on 'Magic Box' by Kit Wright)

I will put in my box . . .
The tail of the most rarest fish
And the shiniest, most beautiful star in the universe,
I will also put in my box . . .
A glow of a fairy and two riddles
One written in Punjabi and one written in Swahili.

I will now put in my box . . .
Queen Elizabeth's first tooth,
And a jewel belonging to an Arabian princess,
Finally, I will add a small bundle of hair
From a girl with silver locks,
And a speck of magic dust that
A maiden has swept away,
The sweetest plum ever and the prettiest dragonfly
Ever to come in front of your eyes,
A jug of water from the Amazon
And finally a snowflake from the North Pole.

My box is made of the coldest ice
It is covered with jewels and it has golden sides,
I will keep my box to myself.

Manreen Pandhal (9)
Manor House School

The Magic Box
(Based on 'Magic Box' by Kit Wright)

I will put in my box . . .
The eyes of frogs
The spaghetti from Bolognese
The brightness of the summer's sun
The singing and dancing of soldiers.

In my box I will put . . .
The leaf of the magic oak tree
The logs of a dragon
The mouth of a chatterbox
The singing of a bird.

My box is made from . . .
Wires, string and snakeskin
The rails of a train
Electric rays (just in case anyone touches it).

I will dance in my box
Dancing or raps and carols
Then chill down in cool showers
And relax on the beach.

Deepika Sondh (10)
Manor House School

The Evil Box

(Based on 'Magic Box' by Kit Wright)

In my box I will put . . .
All the cruelty and darkness in the world,
Black holes with monsters and creatures
That you'd never seen or heard of,
Lord of the Rings, the one ring and
Legolas' bow and arrow.
A dragon's fire and every dragon
From fantasies and nightmares.
My box shall give no mercy to anyone,
For it has Yu-Gi-Oh monsters to rule the world,
If anyone finds this box, evil shall spread,
The monsters shall attack those that have the box,
You have to speak the Elvish language to open it,
It is made out of pure steel,
Covered with crocodiles' skin, dark green,
With magic everywhere you look at it,
It burns you when you touch it,
It is as hot as lava,
Only a human with as much magic can stop its evil,
The box can speak
And make you go crazy.

Sean Zeylmans (10)
Manor House School

Firework Poem

F ireworks are like bombs in the sky,
I nside houses are really dark,
R ocketing into the sky, the starry night,
E xploding high and far,
W on't you stop your banging?
O h please won't you stop that noise?
R oaring all the night,
K icking the sky with your din,
S hooting like a shooting star.

Ryan Bishop (11)
Manor House School

Orange

Orange is the colour of a bright sun
Orange is the colour of a beautiful flower
Orange is the colour of a tiger ready to strike
Orange is the colour of fashionable trainers
Orange is the colour of gangsters' guns ready to kill you
Orange is the colour of delicious juice
Orange is the colour of a shiny rainbow
Orange is the colour of a juicy orange
Orange is the colour of yucky earwax
Orange is the colour of rusty desks
Orange is the colour of 50 Cent's jewellery.

Myles Williams (9)
Manor House School

Fireworks

Fireworks, fireworks, sparkly and bright,
Like World War Three in the middle of the night,
They screech and squeal and make a horrible sound,
Some of them set fire to the ground,
Some of them are dangerous, some of them aren't
And some of them scare my great, great aunt.

Amaechi Obasi (9)
Manor House School

Cars

The Audi is a tough, streetwise person
Never the best, but he'll always survive.

The Aston Martin is a rich, clever businessman,
Living in luxury.

The Mercedes is a big, gunning gangster,
He's rich and is always cool and flashy.

The Rover is a proud war tank,
Everyone thinks it's cool,
But never gets the courage to buy one.

The Ferrari is a champion racehorse,
It's a thoroughbred - it's bound to win!

Adersh Gill (11)
Manor House School

What Is The Earth?

What is the Earth? What is the Earth?
We don't know the meaning of Earth.
The Earth has continents, countries, cities and towns.
It produces flower, grass, fruit and wheat.
It has the rough sea and the calm beaches.
The Earth has chattering children
And gossiping adults.
Earth has beautiful, roaring, small and large animals.
It has fish, dolphins, whales and stinging jellyfish,
In its bright blue sea,
It has birds and volcanoes just waiting to erupt,
The beauty of Earth will always be there.

Simran Tiwana (11)
Manor House School

Sound Poem

The sound of chickens clucking about on the busy farm,
The scratching of a teacher scribbling her thoughts on the board,
An uproaring car revving its engine to the full potential,
A desperate child anxiously rustling through the dictionary
To find the word he is looking for,
A clock ticking in the pure silence.

Jean Cock (11)
Manor House School

The Shrieking Playground

In the playground, you can hear,
Children screaming over a ball,
Teachers trying to call,
To a child who's just been hit,
Shrieking boys having a fit.
Listening to the hubbub rising
Smashing of glasses being thrown,
The dialling of a mobile phone,
The screeching, shrieking of a din
The clumsy clattering of a bin,
The strident shout of a gang of girls fighting
The slow scribble and scratch of others quietly writing.

Jasreen Dhother (10)
Manor House School

In My Box I Will Put

(Based on 'Magic Box' by Kit Wright)

Inside my box I will put . . .
A drop of blood from the last dinosaur that lived,
A splash of water from the Atlantic sea,
And the first present ever given to me.

I will put in my box . . .
Fairy dust only found at the end of the Earth,
Plus a butterfly's wing and the crown of the king.

I will put in my box . . .
A necklace from Princess Diana,
A ring too,
What would you put in your box? It's up to you.

My box is made from
Stars that were ripped out of the sky
And gold from the gold mine.

In my box I will
Go swimming all the time
And watch movies while drinking lemon and lime.

Shauna Kotecha (8)
Manor House School

The Magic Box

(Based on 'Magic Box' by Kit Wright)

I will put in my box . . .

An eyeball from a dragon in Mount Mordor,
The rough skin of a cobra and the toenail of an ogre.

I will put in my box . . .

The most dangerous shark in the Atlantic Ocean and
The horn of the most beautiful unicorn.

I will swim in my box
With all the fishes in the universe.

Maktoum al Maktoum (10)
Manor House School

Football Fireworks

F ireworks are bright
I nce crackles in the night
R obert's whistles as he gets lit
E dilson spins in the air
W illiam's fizzes as he flies past an aeroplane,
O wen dances in the dark
R onaldo flashes as he dances,
K ewell scores - so they blast him off,
S hevchenko shoots faster than a rocket.

Bharat Dhokia (10)
Manor House School

The Magic Box

(Based on 'Magic Box' by Kit Wright)

I will put in my box . . .
The teeth of a Chinese fire-breathing dragon,
A piece of rock on Mount Everest,
The fur of a bear.

I will put in my box . . .
The sound of a piper playing a drum,
The sword of the last Samurai,
The teeth of a sabre-tooth tiger.

I will put in my box . . .
A scale of the rarest snake alive,
The summer season under a green sun,
The wind that blows in the morning.

My box is made of the hardest metal,
Dragon scales,
On the lid I have the spits of a porcupine,
There is an unbreakable code,
Protected by a laser shield.

I shall ride on a dragon in the lands of wisdom
In my box.

Hamzah J Shami (10)
Manor House School

The Magic Box

(Based on 'Magic Box' by Kit Wright)

In my magic box I will put . . .
A red Game Boy Advance SP
A 50 inch plasma screen,
A dinosaur's tooth.

In my magic box I will put . . .
A sharp silver sword
The whole Indian ocean,
A big bit of history.

In my magic box I will put . . .
The skin of a cheetah,
A lab of a brilliant scientist,
A horse of a cowboy.

My box is made of flames
With a moving face which will talk
When an intruder comes.

I shall fly an aeroplane
In the blue sky
Over the wild Atlantic Ocean
And land in a tropical country
With the sun shining down.

Sandeep Sidhu (10)
Manor House School

The Magic Box

(Based on 'Magic Box' by Kit Wright)

In the box I will put . . .
A piece of the world's finest rosewood,
A wing from an angel.

I will put in the box . . .
The coldest icicle from Lapland,
The bright red skin from the oldest dragon,
A golden flash of light from a firework.

I will put in the box . . .
A silky black feather from a blackbird,
A pure white horn from a magical unicorn,
The finest leopard's skin.

I will put in the box . . .
A ray from the blazing sun,
The scales from colourful rainbowfish.

The magical box is made of
The finest gold ever seen,
With the reddest rubies on the lid,
And the greenest emeralds on the sides.

With my box I shall
Paint the most astonishing picture on my wall,
And I shall fly high,
Higher than anyone has ever been with the magic box.

Sareena Samra (9)
Manor House School

Magic Box

(Based on 'Magic Box' by Kit Wright)

I will put in my box . . .
The jewels from a queen's crown shining bright,
Water from the desert, shimmering like mad,
The golden hair from a cowboy.

I will put in my box . . .
Santa Clause with his white curly beard,
A piece of gold from the Golden Temple,
A page from the bible, written in Punjabi.

I will put in my box . . .
The noise of a dolphin after dawn,
The clatter of shoes on the Grand Canyon,
The sour taste of a chocolate.

I will put in my box . . .
Jupiter with a pink sun,
An ant as big as anything,
The Pacific Ocean at Disneyland.

My box is designed with a piece of gold from the North Pole,
The skin of a giraffe at night,
The best rubies ever seen in sight,
Also some emeralds down at the edges.

In my box I shall swim with dolphins till dawn,
Watch the palm trees sway one way,
And see the sunset fall at night.

Sarabjot Tiwana (9)
Manor House School

Fireworks

F laming rockets
I n the air
R iding round the
E lectrical sky
W icked Catherine wheels
O n the gate
R ound and round like a
K amikaze pilot doing
S abotage damage.

Jamie Naylor (11)
Manor House School

Limerick

There once was a lion from Peroose
Who frightened me out of my shoes,
He was big and large
As a garbage barge
And it went on the ITV News.

Miraan Tabrez (9)
Manor House School

The Mermaid's Song

Down, oh so deep,
In the rich ocean sea,
A mermaid sings
Of her melancholy.
She has ruby red lips,
And eyes sapphire blue,
And all of the while she sings of those who
In majestic, strong boats
Pass by and by
With muscular arms
And courageous eye.
She mourns for a sailor
Who will cherish her dearly.
Who will see within her,
Her radiance clearly.
Her search is endless
And still she cries
For one of those sailors,
Who pass heedlessly by.

Aoife Fahy (8)
Pembridge Hall School

My Feelings

Sometimes I'm happy and joyful,
While having lots of fun.

Sometimes I'm sad and angry,
That's when I suck my thumb.

Sometimes I'm frightened of spiders,
I also get very scared.

I wonder what you're scared of?
Perhaps a big, bad bear.

Sometimes I feel annoyed,
Around my sister and brother.

Sometimes I annoy people,
People like my mother.

Those are some of my feelings,
Do you have feelings too?

I think everyone has feelings,
Well, at least I do.

Adelaide Young (9)
Pembridge Hall School

Pirate

My ship is called the Jolly Roger,
But be sure we'll hang every lodger.
My faithful parrot is called Bess,
Everyone she meets will soon be a nasty mess!
I've got a patch and a leg of wood,
I'll cut out your liver if you're not good.
The flag is five drops of blood and a sword,
The first mate on the ship is called Maud
And I nicknamed the brainless cook Fraud!
Me and me mates are fearsome lads,
We even killed our mums and dads!
We've got three prisoners, George, William and James,
We caught them sailing up the River Thames.

Harriet Acland (8)
Pembridge Hall School

Grendel

Where headless creatures lurked and huge rats smirked
There was a swamp where the monster had had a stomp.

As it crawled out of the bog, it even frightened the old warthog,
Said the people of town,
'Tis that thing who knocked our old king's crown.'

Grendel was that monster's name who made the strong
                                        into the lame
He moved around in his lizard-like body, killing
                                and eating anybody
His voice was like the crunching of bones, which he roared
With on a pile of cobwebbed stones.
He had only one eye but he was still a very good spy
His skin was a scaly block of iron and if a
Sword should get into it, it should be as sharp as
                                the tooth of a lion!
A row of razor-sharp spikes went all down his back
(you wouldn't have liked to be given a whack)
To the tip of his tail where a ball of spikes grew,
Each point was as sharp as a dagger for a pirate's crew.
At the end of his knobbly legs were his bony feet,
Now that's not what you want to see walking down the street!
For all that would be left of a man would be a few
                                veins dangling from his jaws.

Jessica Hall (9)
Pembridge Hall School

From Winter To Spring

Looking out onto the empty streets in winter,
No sweet singing from the lark,
A black and white photo you shall see,
Gloomy and faded and dark.

People wrapped up in their coats, all snug,
Sipping hot tea from a mug.
Trees swaying their branches bare
And robins twittering in despair.

But here is *spring*!
Flowers peep shyly out of the soil
And burst into blossom!
Red, blue, green,
What a colourful photo can be seen,
And what with all the light,
Of course soon it will be bright!

Eugenia Pikovsky (8)
Pembridge Hall School

World Of Dreams

When my mum told me to go to bed,
On my cosy pillow I settled my head,
Suddenly dwarves passed by me and
Beside him there was a king.
I heard the lovely mermaid's sing,
The trolls were coming to the land,
Everyone rushed to the golden sand,
The trolls had a fight
And a purple serpent had a bite.
A magical wizard used his lizard,
And then there was a blizzard,
A colourful unicorn came into sight,
And that was the end of the night.

Rosie Stahl (8)
Pembridge Hall School

My Fairyland Dream

I had just fallen asleep in my cosy, soft bed,
With visions of fairies whirling around in my head.
Deep in my dreams,
I found myself riding on a magic, flying horse.
Suddenly we landed and started to trot,
At a gentle, steady course.
We then stopped at a beautiful, green, shimmering place,
I said 'Thank you' to the horse and I set off at a slow pace.
I passed the most magnificent waterfall I had ever seen,
And a fairy's pet mouse whose fur was silky and clean.
I noticed fairies working and flying around,
I saw elves in their gardens digging holes in the ground.
But then I entered into a spooky, dark forest
Where I saw an ogre pulling an elf's nose,
And a witch breaking a wood imp's hose.
But worst of all, I came upon a dragon fast asleep,
So I decided to creep past him without a peep.
It went well at first until I stumbled over a rock and fell.
As the dragon woke in a furious rage,
He jumped at me, blowing fire from his mouth and I really,
Really wished he was in a cage.
I ran in fear screaming, 'Help! Help!'
And once again I tripped and fell with a loud yelp.
I knew the dragon would eat me whole,
And I was a very, very scared soul.
But just as he almost took a bite out of me
I found myself back in bed as happy as could be!

Charlotte de Nassau (8)
Pembridge Hall School

Dreams

When I was asleep in my bed
A dream started performing in my head.
Beautiful winged horses were zooming around
Different coloured dragons started prowling on the ground.
Witches were stirring magic potions,
Ghastly sea monsters were swimming in the oceans.
There were giant mushrooms for fairies to live in
Wizards and trolls were fighting together, wanting to win
Castles on hills were cloaked in mist
Angry trolls were waving their fists.
Soon the dream stopped performing in my head
And then I woke up in my bed.

Katya Pereira (8)
Pembridge Hall School

World Of Dreams

I saw a flowing chocolate stream
I saw it in my dream.

I saw an evil troll
He was sitting by a magical waterfall.

I saw a menacing elf flying around
I saw a flaming hot fire on the ground.

I saw a magic staff
I saw pointy-eared goblins having a laugh.

I saw a colourful mermaid in a river
I saw her come out in a shiver.

I saw a wonderful unicorn
I saw the unicorn had a silver horn.

I saw a dragon's lair
I saw a fairy with long blonde, curly hair.

I saw a mysterious castle
I saw a silver and gold parcel.

I saw poisoned streams
I saw all this in the world of dreams!

Frederique Sleiffer (8)
Pembridge Hall School

My Dream

I saw a huge giant,
I saw a dazzling princess,
I saw a fire-breathing dragon,
I saw a pure white unicorn,
I saw a cruel long-bearded wizard,
I saw a black poisoned pool,
I saw a frightening ogre with green skin,
I saw a small handsome pixie springing through an enchanted forest,
I saw a sword flashing in the moonlight,
I saw a golden wood nymph picking leaves from the magical trees,
I saw a tiny dwarf playing tennis with a sparkling ball,
I saw a magical castle with sparks flying around it,
I saw an enormous troll having a huge feast and drinking red wine,
I saw a snake with a very long tongue.

Rosalie Price (8)
Pembridge Hall School

The Dream

Tonight it's already 8 o'clock,
And the chiming of the clock can't stop
I close my eyes heavily
And dream of sorcery
A cunning princess tying me up to a
Twisted knotted tree,
An elf singing a stupid song comes
Skipping towards me
A misty castle in the sky with
Dragons swooping by
But now I'm awake and I begin to
Quake but I know it was all fake.

Clementine Saglio (9)
Pembridge Hall School

Aliens

Aliens can be blue and red,
Some are rich, some are poor,
Some have a green spiky head,
Some are greedy and always want more.

All aliens are different,
No aliens are the same,
Some have ears that are bent,
And some have no name.

Molly Skinner (9)
Pembridge Hall School

The Land Of Nod

In the land of Nod,
My head was full of pictures which were odd.
I was near a famous castle,
The dwarf was a bit of a rascal.
A beautiful princess was climbing down the castle on air,
But I realised she was going down by her hair.
Then I saw a troll in a poisoned pool,
A little pixie was going to school.
There was a unicorn as white as snow,
A giant glow-worm was aglow.
I was walking by an enchanted river,
There was a dragon eating liver.
I saw some runes carved on trees,
On the branches there were different coloured leaves.
There was a rushing waterfall,
Then I heard someone call.
It was a little gnome that had hurt himself leaping,
Now he was weeping.
Suddenly he stopped crying,
And I thought he was lying.
I went on and saw a mermaid in the sea.
Ow! What just stung me? . . . A bumblebee.
Then in my hand there was a sweet,
I sat upon a sapphire seat.
Then it started to rain,
I licked my candy cane.
The rain smelt like lemon juice,
Something fell on my lap, a tub of chocolate mousse.
I woke up in my bed,
Snuggling my little ted.

Georgia Newell (8)
Pembridge Hall School

Christmas

The bells began to ring.
The choir started to sing.
The Christmas tree glittered.
The red robin twittered.
The pretty snowflakes were falling
On this cold winter's morning.
The sky was filled with delight.
Down below was ever so white.
You could hear the children so jolly.
You could see the prickly, shiny holly.
The stockings were full.
People were wrapped in sheep's wool.
The house was covered in decorations.
It was the best of celebrations.
Children were dancing round the merry tree
Full of happiness and full of glee.
The presents were all wrapped.
The crackers were about to be snapped.
The snow covered the lake.
And all enjoyed the Christmas cake.

Cazalla Fordham (8)
Pembridge Hall School

A Fantasy World

I saw a magical unicorn's golden horn,
I saw a beautiful mermaid's silky hair,
I saw a sweet pixie's little dress torn,
I saw a princess's winged horse sweeping
Through the warm air,
I saw a fairy sprinkling magic dust,
I saw a fortune teller with her crystal ball,
I saw a sword once golden now with rust,
I saw an elf creeping down the castle hall,
In a chamber I saw a goblin outside the
Horrid dragon's poisoned pool,
I saw a shimmering rainbow of gold and silver,
I saw the biggest shining jewel,
I saw a sorcerer's cauldron quiver,
I saw a fantasy world.

Lucia Garnett (8)
Pembridge Hall School

The Sea

At my window I can see
The shining waters of the deep, emerald sea,
The pearly white clouds that seem to dance
In deep romance.
The sand, like a thin sheet of gold,
Being sucked up by the watery deep sea,
And high up I can see the fiery, marigold sun
Sparkling brighter than the brightest flower.
Out in the middle of the ocean,
Dotted around,
Are tiny boats that seem to stay motionless.
As I sit on my chair and see all this beauty
I wish you could see the same as me.

Miranda McEvoy (8)
Pembridge Hall School

The Christmas Present

It was Christmas night,
The snow was still white,
And the sky was still glowing,
It was still snowing.
I heard a sound from downstairs,
I tiptoed towards the tables and chairs,
And there was Santa covered in snow from head to toe.
And then I saw a present in my stocking, it was rocking
And then Santa said to me,
'Ho! Ho! Ho! I really like your tree.'
And then he flew away.
I had nothing more to say,
I climbed into bed,
And lay down my head,
In the morning a robin sang,
The telephone rang,
We all ran to the tree,
We heard a miaow from a gift,
And out of the box, a kitten I lift!

Alessia Miro (8)
Pembridge Hall School

Morning Sounds

Bring, bring, goes my alarm clock in the morning,
And so up I get, still yawning.
Ping goes the toaster down below,
As I hear the postman call, 'Hello!'
My dad is singing in the shower,
Even at such an early hour.
Sizzle, pop, bang go the eggs in the pan,
'Up you get,' calls my gran,
I hear my sister going downstairs,
And I can hear people pulling out their chairs.
Thud, goes the newspaper as it falls to the ground,
These are all the morning sounds!

Chloe McLain (8)
Pembridge Hall School

In Slumberland

In Slumberland
There's boiling blue sand
And a magical ring
Frogs that sing
And trees that twist
And giants' fists
Fairies with pink little shoes
And ogres with pirate tattoos
Glass that melts
And guns that pelt
Blazing fire fountains
And purple-topped mountains
Silver delights
And square snakes that bite
Tiny purple leaves
Swaying blue reeds
Orange and yellow serpents
And a lollipop fence
I must have been dreaming
Through the curtains the sun is now beaming!

Laura Sutcliffe (8)
Pembridge Hall School

The Midnight Garden

The rain is like silver pennies falling from the sky,
The wind is a howling banshee flying through the air,
Busy badgers burrow beneath the broken branches,
Swoosh go the trees as they sway sideways.

Alex Wem (9)
Ravenscourt Park Prep School

The Midnight Garden

The pond swooshed and rippled at night,
The trees breezed silently at midnight,
The multicoloured leaves swirled down from the trees,
Howling of wolves came from nearby,
The grass in the night swayed left and right,
Stars twinkling in the dark, blue sky.
You could hear rain splutter from the gloomy, grey clouds,
It felt like a wonderful place to be.

Alex Fraser (8)
Ravenscourt Park Prep School

The Midnight Garden

Something's stomping on the flowers,
Plodding like an elephant,
Snuffling in the air,
Foxes flee as it comes.
It's scratching on rough bark,
Looks like a big, black hulk with menacing, flashing eyes!
Chomping mouldy cheese!
If you touch it, it feels hairy,
The moon, as bright as a lump of cheese,
Comes out from behind the clouds!
And the big, black, menacing hulk is revealed to be a badger!

Max Carroll-Smith (9)
Ravenscourt Park Prep School

Time

Time goes on and on,
We get older as time goes on,
Things change as time goes on.

People die as time goes on,
People get hurt as time goes on,
Flowers bloom as time goes on,
Seasons come and go as time goes on.

Amy Anderson (9)
Ravenscourt Park Prep School

The Midnight Garden

M um does not know I am here,
I am so scared that I run,
D on't look back,
N ight blinds my eyes.
I hear mice running to their holes,
G hostly shadows slip past me,
H ungry foxes hunt the rabbits,
T he moon glows down on the garden.

G rass swishes in the air,
A s cold as ice.
R oses as dark as the moon,
D ark shadows slowly slip,
E very vine sways in the breeze.
N ight is everywhere.

Jack Fairbairn (8)
Ravenscourt Park Prep School

Midnight Garden

At night when everyone's asleep
When the clock strikes twelve,
Winds as strong as a hurricane sweep across the garden
And now it's midnight.
The dead leaves begin to rustle
When the racoons forage for food.
The sweet scent of the roses dying down
When the squirrels hunt nuts.

And foxes come and *pounce* on rabbits
And other predators.
The flowers are closing their petals,
The blossoms with their blend of red and purple.
Oh no, the clock has struck six,
It has to transform into a normal garden.

Amy Taylor (9)
Ravenscourt Park Prep School

My Midnight Garden

M y midnight garden is all quiet and dark,
I rises growing to be a surprise in the morning,
D own beneath the earth, the foxes are trying to sleep.
N othing is making a sound except crickets croaking in the grass.
I n the distance, wolves are howling up at the bright, shining moon.
G eese are flying to and fro from the cool pond.
H eavy clouds surround the moon and make it shine bright.
T omorrow in the sun, the irises will be ready
  and the foxes will be gone.

Alex Sanderson (8)
Ravenscourt Park Prep School

My Midnight Garden

My midnight garden is heaven,
You can see the moon glow like a meteor,
You can hear the howling wolves howl for some prey,
The crickets chirp like a broken alarm,
The smell of chocolate in the oven wafts through the air.
You see the foxes and badgers search for food in the bins,
In the night you hear the wind,
Whistling, swooshing, rippling,
That's my midnight garden
That I will keep for ever and ever.

Thanos Samaras (8)
Ravenscourt Park Prep School

The Midnight Garden

Daffodils gently sway in the wind,
No sound is made,
Foxes crawl on the floor,
Rustling the leaves around
The dark place
Lit by the moon
As sleek as stars.
There is no sound,
Birds are sleeping
In their nests to keep warm and dry.
No splashing comes from the pond,
Ducks sleep silently over in a hut nearby,
Eyes sparkling in the dark,
Twinkling like stars when the moon shines above.
In the distance a clock
Chimes twelve.
Bang, bang twelve times.
It's midnight in the garden
When the clock chimes.

Charlotte Guffick (8)
Ravenscourt Park Prep School

The Midnight Garden

The moon lights up the garden as the foxes empty the bin,
The ground glows in the moon's rays, as white as shiny tin.

A rustle in the grass
As a snake makes a pass.

A badger, one or two,
The silent snore of a cuckoo.

The cats are fighting
As fast as lightning.

The bats
Are watching the cats.

The owls are looking for food as they fly,
So they can make a dormouse into a pie.

But soon they will all be going to sleep,
As the sun first makes its peep.

Ned Thomas (9)
Ravenscourt Park Prep School

My Secret Garden

The sweet smell of roses wafted through the air.
The trickle of the water fountain stopped as the clock chimed
twelve times.
Little, rusting animals' feet stopped and once more silently took over.
The moon bathed in the shadows of the night sky.
The wind eased its way through the trees like a herd of horses.
Velvety petals all spread on the floor as summer turned to autumn
and flowers died once more.

Leaves dropped off the flowers and the sweet scents died away.
The moon still glowed like a large torch in the sky.
The golden brown and red leaves dropped from the trees spreading all
over the garden like a large blanket.
The wind howled down your ear and a shiver ran down your spine.
The chilling feel of water running down your throat like swimming in
a rapid river.

When winter came, the frost spread and took over the life that used
to remain.
The snowdrops spread over the cold, still ground like the sun over
the world.
Winds rapidly rushed through hair, gusts of wind pelted from
all directions.
All green was now brown and holly trees were placed everywhere.
The trees echoed like they were growling at the sun as the snow
buried them in a warm blanket.

Cockleshells formed now it was spring and daffodils started to
form on the ground.
The sweet lambs and young rabbits were born and birds sang
in delight.
The gusts of wind were gone and the sun tried to shine out from
hiding under the clouds.
The flowers started to bloom and colour spread throughout the
garden.
The stream was not ice and the lambs were born.

Ali Sermol (9)
Ravenscourt Park Prep School

The Midnight Garden

At night in the secret garden the crickets are chirping,
The smell of the mould from the walls rising through the air,
The moon will get clearer and clearer and clearer,
The rain gets heavier and heavier.
The walls rot more and more,
The ground gets covered with leaves,
The mud gets sprayed by the wind,
You could trip on the fallen trees
Or get a fright and think some holly is a bullet.
The rust uncovers and reveals the stars.
There is a fountain with the most fresh water you will ever taste,
And that's what happens in the secret garden.

Tom Austin (9)
Ravenscourt Park Prep School

The Midnight Garden

Twi, twi, twi, twi, twi, twi, twi, twi, twi, twi, twi, twi,
Midnight had come, I hadn't shut my eyes,
Slowly, silently, I slithered to the ground.

Foxes everywhere, out of the den.
An owl howled like a wolf sliding in the sky.
Past me went the snake, hissing in the dark.

The wind rushed through branches, moaning as it went,
Little beast awoke, small eyes fixed on me.
I couldn't bear it, it terrified me!

Slugs, snails were out at the time
At which I was there,
But I didn't notice them because bats were there!

Spiders were there too, like dancers on the ropes,
Snakes were cords, designed to climb on.
To them be the victim, the victim of their trap.

Boom!
Something had fallen there, and here as well!
What was it? Whatever it was, this garden was
            Hell!

Julia Maillard (9)
Ravenscourt Park Prep School

The Midnight Garden

The midnight garden, creepy and still,
as cold as the Atlantic Ocean.
Damp dew dangles from the flower bed.
The trickling river washes the wet banks,
all the owls are going *tu-whit tu-whoo.*
Their screech is an eerie blast.

All the foxes come out to hunt,
their tiny feet going 'pitter-patter'.

The gloomy, dark, glorious moon shines upon you.
Suddenly all the animals go, *boom, crash, hiss, woof, whoo!*

The green, green grass grows up the wall
and as tall as an oak tree
and is frog green.
Suddenly all the animals go, *boom, crash, hiss, woof, whoo!*

Ross Bernard (9)
Ravenscourt Park Prep School

The Midnight Garden

One night I heard a noise
so I got out of bed,
I opened up my bedroom door,
fell over and banged my head.

I went outside to check the noise
to find it was dark.
I went to the garage to get a torch
and heard a dog bark.

I went up to the garage
and slipped inside.
I saw something furry,
it was animal hide.

It then made a noise,
the noise was *moo.*
I went back a little
and realised I'd stepped in its poo.

I wondered why it was here,
this isn't a farm.
Anyway if it was,
it should be in the barn.

My search took me further
into the night,
I heard an owl whooing,
it gave me a fright.

Other animals gathered around me,
lit up by the moon.
Sheep and goat and pigs were there,
others were there soon.

The animals started intensely at me,
questions in their eyes,
They seemed to befriend me,
there was no element of surprise.

I promised all the animals
to find them all each night.
I left the garden quickly
and shut the great door tight.

Theo Rigden (9)
Ravenscourt Park Prep School

The Midnight Garden

O'er the garden shadows gently steal,
All is silent at last,
The moon gives off a silvery light,
Its lovely beam is vast.

Foxes creep! Their ghostly figures
Slinking so stealthily in the dark,
Keeping to hedgerows, ever so quiet,
So the house dogs will not bark.

Owls hunt and hoot,
What was that?
They hunt for mice
And starve the cat.

Leaves float down
Making a silent duvet for my den,
It will still be there when I wake up
For me to clear away again.

Zoë Ashford (8)
Ravenscourt Park Prep School

The Midnight Garden

M y garden swaying in the dark,
I n the moonlight it shines like a bright, bright sun,
D ogs barking and lights all around,
N o one knows where my garden is,
I t's all quiet, only a cricket you hear,
G inormous bugs hiding in the trees,
H eavy stones slipping down a river,
T ortoises moving very slowly,

G iant fish swimming in the pond,
A great owl hooting in the moonlight,
R ipe apples you cannot see,
D elightful daisies, roses and daffodils,
E ven tulips moving slightly in the wind,
N ight is wonderful in my garden, silent as a mouse
    graceful swans, beautiful butterflies and now no one
    coming near.

Serena Steptoe (8)
Ravenscourt Park Prep School

The Midnight Garden

The snakes slithered through the silky, slimy door,
The trees were swaying to and fro.
Bang! The birds fluttered as quickly as they could,
I saw a particular star in the sky and I made a wish,
It was that I had a proper family.

The owls hooted and the birds were chirping,
The squirrels went up the tree for safety and for resting,
The fish went into their homes and slept like children,
We were beneath them, somewhere safe.

Ravi Patel (8)
Ravenscourt Park Prep School

Panda

I eat bamboo all day and night,
but sometimes I have to put up a fight
against leopards and deer.
You know I nearly lost an ear.
I like to climb up tall, big trees,
but the trouble is they make me sneeze.
My extra thumb is useful
for eating my bamboo.
But what is even more tasty
is my lovely bamboo stew.

Hugh Crawshaw (8)
Ravenscourt Park Prep School

The Midnight Garden

It was dark and scary in the midnight garden,
the moon was a huge, clear, shiny diamond.
When I woke up in my soft bed,
I heard an owl going *woo, woo!*
I looked out of my dusty window,
I saw the garden shimmering
like the shimmering sun.
I opened my bedroom door,
it creaked open silently.

I tiptoed past my mum's bedroom,
'Miaow!'
It was only the cat.
I walked into the sparkling midnight garden.
The damp grass was cold
and it was like walking on ice.
The branches on the trees were like
a box of chocolates.

The flowers were drooping
like people sleeping.
The garden was different in a way.
The sun doesn't shine
in the garden in the day!
Only the shimmering moon makes
the garden as dark as gloom!

Lexie Drijver (9)
Ravenscourt Park Prep School

The Midnight Garden

Tick-tock, tick-tock, tick-tock, tick-tock, tick-tock, tick-tock,
Tick-tock, tick-tock, tick-tock, tick-tock, tick-tock, tick-tock,
It was midnight!
Pitter-patter, pitter-patter went the rain on the greenhouse roof,
Crash! It was the big old birch that had just been snapped
in half by the howling wind.
The wind howled like a wolf howling at the moon.
The silver, shimmering moon shone onto the silent deserted garden.
The snake slithering silently along the path is a stick
being blown about by a breeze.
The gold and silver fish swimming under the fountain
were sweets' wrapping paper.
The furtive, fluffy fox followed the footsteps of its prey.
The cat miaowed mournfully like a wailing baby.

Erin Blackmore (8)
Ravenscourt Park Prep School

The Midnight Garden

My midnight garden is revealed when the moon is shining bright,
It calls owls in circling flight quietly as a breeze at night.
My shadow dances in the warm firelight,
My feet in the twilight give a soft little crack,
Now I tiptoe to my bed and rest my solid head
And dream about my midnight garden,
Sometimes there but rarely seen.

Seth Aronsohn
Ravenscourt Park Prep School

The Vampires Kill

In the darkness where the vampires lay
They saw badness in the hay.
The Devil lay in the hay while laughing up above.
They sucked the people's blood in the moonlight before sunrise,
The bodies were crushed and smashed and gushing with blood,
The vampires were left to rest until the next night.
Now the moonlight went away.

Kia Dickinson (9)
Ravenscourt Park Prep School

That Is What Goes On At Midnight

The moon shines like smelly cheese,
As the clock strikes twelve it becomes midnight,
Foxes jump around in bins and boxes,
All the cats slithering around and going *miaow!*
And the owls perching on trees and going *hoot!*
Some stray dogs walking along the streets go *woof!*
That is what goes on at midnight.

People snoring, people snoozing as they sleep,
People walking down the street, not knowing where they're going,
Clocks bonging, winds blowing all over the town,
Grass swishing, trees swooshing all over the park,
That is what goes on at midnight.

Nick Learoyd (8)
Ravenscourt Park Prep School

The Midnight Garden

I hear foxes rustling in the breeze,
I watch the moonlight shining in the trees,
The place is dark and damp as the clock chimes twelve.
The wolves howl as sad as a cry,
The moon is like a football,
The swings sway silently in the breeze.
It is as dark as a graveyard.
The leaves rustle and the wind blows,
The rain blows hard,
It is dark at night, very dark.

Robbie Burnett (8)
Ravenscourt Park Prep School

The Midnight Garden

My midnight garden has many surprises.
Two gloomy eyes gleam like green lights,
two grey arms as a grey cloud covers the moon,
black figure disappears in the night sky.

Shadows appear in the garden,
they take shape by the black sky,
other shapes take place by the ivy on the wall.
But those shadows fall
and now happiness spreads
through the garden.

Enrico Dal Cin (9)
Ravenscourt Park Prep School

The Midnight Garden

The smell of daffodils wafted away in the wind,
The moon watched gloomily down upon the green trees,
Swinging ivy with fierce shadows swaying
On the soft, soggy, silky grass.
The distant sounds of wolves howl at the cheesy moon,
Chirping crickets as loud as disco music,
The fountain made no noise except for the
    splash of the water which was as silver as metal.

Jack Pilgrem (8)
Ravenscourt Park Prep School

The Midnight Garden

The garden bathed in moonlight,
At first it gave me quite a fright
And then it seemed quite
A spooky sight to see.
I saw some creeper hanging from the wall,
I didn't like the look of it at all.
A tree stood in front of me
It looked like it could see,
I turned and fled, running out flat,
I learned from that,
Never go into a garden at midnight,
Otherwise you might die of fright.

Daniel Hart (9)
Ravenscourt Park Prep School

The North Wind Doth Blow

The creaking of the door
The howling of the wind
The pounding of the sea
The crying of the children and
The cawing of the birds
Echo in my head.

Antonia Blakeman (9)
Ravenscourt Park Prep School

Going Over The Top

I heard the first call
I went outside
I heard the second
I heard the whistle
I went over
It smelt like smoke
I saw the machine gun
I heard people crying
I tasted blood
I felt my gun
I felt the bullet go through me
I fell to the floor
I stared at the sky
I could not move
I shouted, 'Help!'

Tristan Beney (8)
Ravenscourt Park Prep School

The Midnight Garden

The grass was a green mask melting in the soft soil,
The water fountain glowed like the moon over a spoon.
The flower bed had a bear called Ned.
The tree had a bee on the branch, buzzing from flower to flower.
The fountain dropped a drop of water, down and down, and then,
pitter-patter, the water had sunk into the soft soil.
The mountain in the background was a hard rock in the middle
of a round river.
The mountain munched the multicoloured flowers,
The wind was a piece of wobbly wire swinging higher and higher.

Hannah Myers (8)
Ravenscourt Park Prep School

The England Rugby Team

Jonny Wilkinson scoring, New Zealand ignoring,
Martin Johnson scrumming, New Zealand drumming,
Jason Robinson sprinting, England winning,
Josh Lucy kicking, New Zealand missing,
Joy in my heart at the cheering,
Martin Johnson got a try, New Zealand did not know why.

Sacha Shilov (9)
Ravenscourt Park Prep School

Dangerous Animals

Animals can be dangerous and bad,
They also can be very sad,
They are sad to be trapped in the zoo,
They can even be good lads.

A cheetah can make a stew
That is made of you,
Its birthday is in June
And is trained to go to the loo.

A frog's favourite food is prunes,
They also love funny tunes,
They are also very dumb,
They mostly live in a lagoon.

A peacock can do a sum,
They can also say 'Yum,'
They can give you a knock,
They can also chew gum.

A shark can eat your sock,
They can even undo a lock,
They can swim to the North Pole,
They can even swallow a rock.

Animals are poor souls,
There are monkeys, whales and moles,
Be careful if they fall in holes,
They can even look like dolls.

Ata Bastami (8)
Ravenscourt Park Prep School

Rainfall

The pitter-patter of the rain,
Drumming at my window,
This is fun watching the rain spread around the place,
It's like tears of joy on someone's face.

Drip drop drip,
The rain sounds like,
But it means more to me.

It means
Someone has great news,
It means some one is crying,
It means people have water to drink,
That's what rain means to me.

Love is around,
People are together,
They will be for ever,
Rain is great sometimes,
But not all the time.

We will be together,
When the rain is here,
Rain is best,
Rainfall.

Luke Rosher (11)
St Mary Abbots CE Primary School

Super School

In the classroom
Children chatting at the desks
Some are reading some are not
All are having fun!

In the playground
Boys bouncing basketballs
Girls are skipping, some are shouting
It is very noisy!

At PE
Ralph runs rapid races,
We're all playing catch,
We have a good time!

In the hall
Teachers telling tales
Some are talking, some are not,
The assembly has begun!

I love my super school!
In the classroom, very hot,
In the playground, very cold,
At PE we learn to play,
In the hall we learn some more!

Ana-Victoria Dan (11)
St Mary Abbots CE Primary School

Tiger

Teeth like daggers, being set a task,
The creature moves slowly through the grass,
He cunningly moves as if not to be shown,
Maybe because he has secrets not to be known . . .

The mind is focused,
The eyes are still
He has a plan
There is a chill . . .

He has the strength that he keeps for long
He has the mind to know that nothing is wrong.

The sun hides
The moon screams
The tiger roars with a deadly gleam . . .

Caspian Whistler (10)
St Mary Abbots CE Primary School

The Night Is A Safe Harbour

The night is a safe harbour,
Warm and snug it be,
Like the hands of God holding me from fears,
Or surrounded by comforting trees.

The day is a trusty healer,
Although not a doctor it be,
It's a cheerful, bright time with no tears,
And a smile, that's what it puts on me.

The school is a kind helper,
Helps you learn with your jobs to be,
Everyone helps like a friend for you,
It always works for me.

Ralph Soberano (11)
St Mary Abbots CE Primary School

The Red Shoes - A Calligram

My feet move
to the beat.
My arms sway
to the song.
My heart plays
the song.
But my feet
carry on.
My body
moves to
the song.
But still the tune carries on.
I keep going but my feet feel bruised.
But still my red shoes tap to the tune.
I feel a bang just as the orchestra starts another song.
But still   my red shoes carry on.
Up to heaven   I sing this song. but still
My red shoes   c a r r y   o n . . .

Nancy Andersen (11)
St Mary Abbots CE Primary School

Stairway To Heaven

As we wind on down the road
Our shadows taller than our souls
There walks a lady we all know
Who shines white and wants to show
How everything still turns to gold
And if you listen very hard
The tune will come to you at last
As all is one and one is all
For that spirit to enter our soul;
As we still walk on
We hear a song
That we will live for ever
If we live and work together.
We were all born gifted
But we did not know the gifts were here to use
We wonder why our souls were lifted
Our holy hearts would start to cry
As we learned to kill and lie.
But He will forgive
So we will live
As we get tempted by the serpent
He will ask us to repent.
We still have not reached our destination
But we will if we avoid temptation
Until we see a shadow
We did not know
To give our love and let it show
To cleanse our hearts and let them glow.
We hear a voice, very loud that He will be proud,
Once again we see the serpent
We change the side and go to where we are sent.
A shining light
Will blind our sight
As we see the holy gate
It looks so big, so great
We reach our destination
To live by God and avoid temptation.

Jovan Grbic (10)
St Mary Abbots CE Primary School

The Night Is A Safe Harbour

The night is a safe harbour,
Just like some person's home,
To a bird it's a paradise,
To a person it's so alone.

The night is a safe harbour,
Where boats rest for the night,
The sky is a velvet cover,
And the moon is their light.

The night is a safe harbour,
Cabins all over,
People in slumber
In their blankets of clover.

The night is a safe harbour . . .

Jake Pummintr (11)
St Mary Abbots CE Primary School

The Night Is Count Dracula

The night is Count Dracula,
Screaming to find his next victim.
His black coat covers the city
His fangs pierce my skin.

He's near
In your future coffin
He lies awake
Waiting for you . . .

Waiting!

Jessica Cherag-Zade (10)
St Mary Abbots CE Primary School

The Stormy Night

One dark autumn night,
The full moon was hiding,
I heard the wind moan
And I felt the sea rising

I snatched my blanket
I crept down the stairs
As quickly as could be
And ran to the sea.

The waves threw me high,
And crashed me down low,
I almost lost track
Of which way to go.

An island grew closer
'Row hard,' I told Ted.
'It's getting much bigger,
It's just up ahead.

We're there!'

I heard a few sniffles,
Then somebody sneezed,
And a tearful old rabbit
Hopped out of the trees.

Skunks, squirrels, rabbits,
Birds, otters and deer
Were all huddled together
And shaking with fear.

First we needed a shelter
From this dark, stormy sky.
We needed to build something
To keep us all dry.

Amal Jebari (10)
St Mary Abbots CE Primary School

The Night Is A Safe Harbour

The night is a safe harbour,
And I, a ship,
In my soft bed, so downy and soft,
I pull up the anchor and I'm off!

Up in my little ship of dreams,
Up where the night is not where it seems,
The velvety darkness will keep me warm,
And the moon's kindly face will keep me safe till dawn.

The curtains flapping at my window,
The moon looking down on an adult to be,
The night is a safe harbour,
And will always be safe to me.

Zoe Gordon (10)
St Mary Abbots CE Primary School

Gigantic Giant

People look up to the gigantic giant
He looks down on them
And on their houses that are just matchboxes
To him and
No one knows *why!*

The mouse holes hidden in secret places
The mice smaller than ants
In giants' eyes
Finally faint, flimsy figures fluttering like
Butterfly wings until they stop.

The giant has gone to sleep.

Chevez Bouaita (10)
St Mary Abbots CE Primary School

The Giant

A house like a Lego cube,
The tiniest toy I know.
The population like a colony of ants,
The minuscule mass of people.
The skyscraper like a molehill
Dominating the dashing skyline.
The clouds like a blanket beneath my feet,
Tickling and teasing my toes,
The sea like a steaming bath,
The soothing of my senses.
The underground like a train set,
The system running smoothly.

Max Brewer (10)
St Mary Abbots CE Primary School

I Used To

I used to play with the little toys
The cuddly toys and the pretend oven
I used to follow people about
I'm too old for the young and too young for the old.

I used to copy my auntie
Whatever she did I did
I liked party games and clowns
I'm too old for the young and too young for the old.

I'm over that, I've done it all
But now there's nothing to do
I'm too old for the young and too young for the old.

Zack Harris (11)
St Mary Abbots CE Primary School

The Night Is Count Dracula

He unlocks the window with his nail
And bites into my throat.
I try to scream but terror takes the sound
Out of my throat
Before I am ready to make it.
My blood turns cold and my skin turns pale
My eyes open wide with fear.
He sucks life out of my body.
The night
Count Dracula.

Jack Edgington (10)
St Mary Abbots CE Primary School

Rainbow

The rainbow rained across the sea
Like bright colours dropping from
The light blue sky
With the blood-red of roses
And the violet of freshly crowned tulips
With the yellow of new daisies
And the blue of soundless bluebells
The colours of the rainbow are as light and
Delicate as hummingbirds
The colours of the rainbow are unique
As I watch them glittering and fluffing up
Their sparkling feathers across the sky . . .

Amara O'Donoghue (11)
St Mary Abbots CE Primary School

Pollution

Will they ever change their ways,
And love me as much as gold?
Each day I cry out to be cared for and loved as much as silver.

Pollution, it's a nasty thing,
If only people knew what they were doing to me.
One day I will be gone!
Then people will say, 'What have we done?'

For I am the world, I cry out to be heard,
For one day I will be *gone, gone, gone, gone, gone.*

Albert Berchie (11)
St Mary Abbots CE Primary School

The Night Is Dracula

Dracula has come,
Trees are crashing,
Dracula has come.
I hear him say, 'You are next.'
I hide in the corner,
Dracula has come.
With my cover over me
I feel his breath,
I hope to go to the next world,
Dracula has come.
I try to scream
But it is too late,
The night is over.

Sayo Akinlude (11)
St Mary Abbots CE Primary School

Some Day

Some day we will be back
Nobody can shift me till death me part.
This is my home, my kingdom, this is where
I was born, this is where I shall die.
We need no help just me and
Catherine, we shall make it,
We shall make it back home where we belong.

We shall fight till we have won,
We cannot lose, we need no help.
We shall succeed.

Some day we will be back,
Some day we will be *back*.

Anthony Haswell-Sewell (10)
St Mary Abbots CE Primary School

Eris To Serycus

To kill them Eris, goddess of death
Verses
Serycus and the book of peace.

Serycus . . . Eris
Fit lose . . . Darius
The book of peace
Your love may cease
Against the evil Eris.

The Eris dwells on your love
To what may be above
The land of death.

The world roars *'Ahhh'*
The world goes far
For what might torture us.

Tarturas oh tartaras
The land of death awakes
And kills what might be men.

The sirens kill the nasty men
To bring them death
But women stay aware
Of what might bring a stare
To all mankind.

But Serycus is the land of hope
Holding the book of peace
But Eris
But   Eris
But   Eris
But   Eris
But   Eris
Eris
Eri
Er
E

Brings death to all living men
And steals the book of peace
To bring all men cease
To bring all men cease

Natasha El Zein (10)
St Mary Abbots CE Primary School

Death

White is for alive,
Black is for death,
Go to . . .
Explore the dark
In the darkest and deepest dungeon.

You will see a shadow
Talk to him, he will ask,
'How did you die?'
And you will feel the death, all cold and dry,
You will be dead in a second
And then you will feel no more . . .

Enkhluun Enkhmandakh (11)
St Mary Abbots CE Primary School

Giraffe

The giraffe is . . .
Like a children's climbing frame
Made with bamboo sticks.
Like scaffolding propped against a wall
With a ladder reaching up to the sky
With yellow and brown spots.

Jonathan Ordonez (10)
St Mary's School, Hammersmith

My Excuses

(Based on 'Excuses, Excuses' by Gareth Owen)

'Late again, Louise?
What's your excuse this time?'
'Well, Dad's car broke down, Sir,'
'What do you mean your dad's car broke down?'
'The engine broke, Sir.'
'Well then, have you brought your homework in?'
'No Sir.'
'Where is it?'
'In the car, Sir.'
'Why?'
My brother, Tyrel took my pencil case Sir.'
'Okay, it's time for your swimming money, Louise.'
'Sorry Sir, I don't have it.'
'Why don't you have it?'
'I left it in my pencil case, Sir.'
'I am fed up with hearing your excuses!'

Annakai Brown (10)
St Mary's School, Hammersmith

The Bear

The bear is . . .
Dirty snow that has been trampled on,
With paws as sharp as a needle.
A mega-sized football of fur
That can't be kicked.
A brown, hairy carpet
And chocolate-flavoured ice cream.
The bear is like a podgy tree trunk
That can travel from place to place.

Stephanie Kattah (10)
St Mary's School, Hammersmith

Dolphin

You move like a spring jumping in and out of the crumpled sea,
Then your triangular fin moves slowly above the water.
Your back is like an old man bending on his walking stick,
Your silk skin is like a diamond glistening on my hand,
And you're as loveable as my cuddly toy lying on my bed.
Your beautiful voice is like my high heels clicking fast on the floor
And your voice creates the waves across the sea.

Jasmine Ruske (10)
St Mary's School, Hammersmith

Excuses, Excuses, It's Always Excuses

(Based on 'Excuses, Excuses' by Gareth Owen)

'Late again, John! Why were you late?'
'I lost my brain, Sir.'
'Where is it?'
'In the freezer, Sir.'
'In the freezer? What is it doing there?'
'I don't know, Sir.'
'Why are your clothes wet?'
'I was in the washing machine, Sir.'
'The washing machine? Why?'
'Because my clothes were stuck onto me.'
'Why are your clothes creased?'
'Not ironed, Sir.'
'Why not lad?'
'The person who does it is in hospital.'
'Who was it?'
'My mum, Sir.'
'Your mum?'
'Yes, Sir.'
'Why is she in hospital?'
'Fainted, Sir.'
'Where is your PE kit?'
'In the swimming pool, Sir.'
'Why?'
'Because a shark came out and put it in, Sir.'
'Excuses, excuses, excuses don't you ever tell the truth?'

Akosua Achiaa (10)
St Mary's School, Hammersmith

The Hare

You're like a fluffy spring
And a furry pencil case.
Your ears are like two tall triangles.
You bounce all day and
You bounce all night,
You bounce in the dark
And you bounce in the light.
Your tail is like candyfloss
And your legs are like two big sticks,
You're like a colourful bouncy ball
And you're like a cloud with legs.

Josephine Kiernan (10)
St Mary's School, Hammersmith

My Excuses

(Based on 'Excuses Excuses' by Gareth Owen)

'Late again David,
What's the excuses this time?'
'I was burgled, Sir.'
'So why didn't you call the police?'
'My phone broke.'
'Right, time for RE,'
'Can't do it Sir.'
'Why not?'
'No pencil case Sir.'
'Where is it?'
'In my bag Sir.'
'So go and get it.'
'Can't Sir.'
'Why not?'
'The burglar stole it sir.'

Jan Zanato (10)
St Mary's School, Hammersmith

The Cat

Your nails are like sharp needles
Fur like velvet,
You scratch like a fierce cheetah
And your tail is like a snake
You are a big, fat fur ball
As well as being extremely cunning like a fox
Your eyes are brighter than two lasers
When you purr it sounds like an engine running.

Rebecca Vukic (9)
St Mary's School, Hammersmith

The Snow White Kitten

You, snow white gentle animal
Curled up like your own blanket.
You jump like acrobat and
You are like a fluffy pencil case.
I see you as white candyfloss and
Your smile is like a baby laughing.

Shannon Flynn-Constant (9)
St Mary's School, Hammersmith

Crocodile

You are camouflage like green grass.
Your teeth are like pencils' leads.
Your back is like a mountain.
You snap like a crab's claw.
You are king of the water.
Your eyes are like the sun.

Arran Farrell (10)
St Mary's School, Hammersmith

The Crocodile

The crocodile is . . .
Big as a jet plane,
Built like a wrestler,
Fearless as a lion,
Cunning as a fox,
Silent as a burglar and
Its skin is as tough as steel
His colour is green as green can be
He is also a deadly predator to us all.

Ryan Moultesz (10)
St Mary's School, Hammersmith

Polar Bear

There you are,
In your white fluffy coat.
I see you as a piece of pure white paper,
You remind me of clouds on a sunny day.
You walk like a shaking baby
Crawling on a rough surface,
When you look after your cubs
You're a mother looking after her baby.
You're like the invisible man against the white snow.

Amy O'Callaghan (10)
St Mary's School, Hammersmith

Mr Twit

Mr Twit, you may have heard,
Likes eating pies with lots of birds.
He catches them with sticky glue,
But once a big bird told them 'Shoo!
Go go! Fly high! Or you'll end
Up in a hot bird pie!'

When Mr Twit awoke looking like a mouse,
He said, 'Oh poohy! They're on the roof.
Mrs Twit come on let's get some guns,
Then we can shoot right through their lungs!'
But when the Twits came back with a scowl,
The birds had turned the house upside down.

The Twits walked in then got their head stuck,
The birds cheered, 'What bad luck!'
'Oh no,' they cried, 'I've got the shrinks.'
Then Mr Twit shouted, 'Jinks!'

Leila Tompkins (8)
St Peter's CE Primary School, Hammersmith

Bungee-Jumping Leaves

Bungee-jumping leaves
        Bouncing off trees.
          Making whirlpools
    Swirling and dancing
Being flattened by the tyres
       Then being picked up by the light breeze!

Wallis Gray (8)
St Peter's CE Primary School, Hammersmith

My Midnight Unicorn

It was night
I saw a light
It was a bright light
And it gave me a fright
I looked out of the window
And guess what I saw
My midnight unicorn lying still on the floor.

Rosemary Morgan (8)
St Peter's CE Primary School, Hammersmith

Early One Morning . . .

My husband died yesterday,
How could he?
He promised he was here to stay.
Well, it was my fault, you see
It was a little argument, between him and me.
He wanted to go to Burger King, I thought McDonald's was better,
I stabbed him in the back with the knife we used for spreading butter.
I wish I hadn't, I loved that knife, it's all bent now,
Why was I such a rotten cow?
Today was his funeral, I wasn't welcome there,
I was his wife, life isn't fair!

Camille Biddell (10)
St Peter's CE Primary School, Hammersmith

The Animal

He lay asleep on the tree,
I could see freedom in his eyes,
He looked very sad,
I came back the next week and he still lies.

I knew the animal wanted his mother,
By the way he hung his head down low,
I wish I could set him free,
He kept on swinging very slow.

Edward Letch (9)
St Peter's CE Primary School, Hammersmith

Gorilla

A gorilla sat staring into space,
His straggly black hair was matted and unkempt,
His round black glassy eyes were staring at a crowd
                                    beginning to gather.
Children laughed and jeered ungratefully at the sorry sight,
Only one small girl felt sorry for the gorilla deep down in her heart.
Her wide blue eyes were fixed on him and a teardrop began to fall.
The gorilla watched her pressing his face against the glass
Trying to touch her, but he could not because the glass was in the
way.

Imogen Newton (9)
St Peter's CE Primary School, Hammersmith

Why?

Why did I have to climb that tree?
Why did I fall and cut my knee?
Why was I there when they let the net fall?
Why am I here doing nothing at all?
Why has cage life driven me mad?
Why do I now have a feeling so sad?
Why am I not where I used to be?
Why am I not walking, running, swinging,
Jumping, rolling, strolling happily free?

Emma Tanner (10)
St Peter's CE Primary School, Hammersmith

The Fish!

I was swimmin' around
Under the ground,
Then I was found.
I was made into a dish,
Because I was a fish,
There was blood everywhere
But I didn't care,
I didn't have a head,
Because I was dead,
I didn't cry because I wasn't alive!

Ella Frosdick (9)
St Peter's CE Primary School, Hammersmith

The Alien

An alien came from outer space
To try and stop the human race,
He was green and blue and very blobby,
His knees and elbows were both knobbly.
I went to him and said, 'Hello, you look like a nice fellow.'
Then I said, 'You're a beast,
You can tell me where you're from at least!'
I walked away, he wouldn't talk, anyway I needed a walk.

Thomas Kaplan (9)
St Peter's CE Primary School, Hammersmith

Animals In Captivity

What are these bars in front of me for?
Where are the leaves that I so much adore?
I want to roam the plains,
Not have all these achy pains.

I want my family, I want them now.
How did they get away, how, how?
I don't like my keeper he's really bad,
Oh I know the whole world's gone mad!

Where's the lake I used to bathe in?
I like the salmon, just not from a tin.
Why do I have to live in the zoo?
Why, why, *nooo!*

Samuel Kaplan (9)
St Peter's CE Primary School, Hammersmith

I Shouldn't Be Here!

They captured me,
Those killing machines,
Now I'm locked in bars,
Bars of an everlasting prison.

Where is my home?
And my mum
The waterhole I first lapped water from,
And the place I'm meant to be.

My paws are burning,
I see blurs from my eyes,
Anger, rage,
A leopard shouldn't be here.

Polly Kaplan (9)
St Peter's CE Primary School, Hammersmith

Magic Dragons

Red and black dragon
Fly through the misty sky
His wings fly so high
Knights fight the horrible beasts
Then they go for a big feast
After they have filled their bellies
They go to sleep on a bed of straw
And dream of dragons' roar.

James Lovelidge (9)
St Stephen's CE Primary School, Westminster

Ghosts

My teacher is a ghost,
And she never goes out for her toast,
I told her what to say,
But she was on her summer bay.

Rumi Shanina Islam (9)
St Stephen's CE Primary School, Westminster

The Queen

The Queen thinks she's posh but is really an old bag,
She's old and wrinkly and must be a nag.
The Queen thinks she's flash,
'Cause she's loaded with cash.
The Queen doesn't have any fashion,
But I've got to admit, is full of passion.
She's one I've never seen,
Yes, the Queen!

Shaince Gray (9)
St Stephen's CE Primary School, Westminster

The Lord Of The Rings Poem

Slice the Orcs and chop their heads, kick them down into a pit
Aragorn he is so cool, he likes to swim in a swimming pool
Legolas, he is so mean, his favourite colour is so green
Gimli he is so small, he will never get to be so tall
Gandalf is very white and he is very bright
Samwise is very brave, he would even walk into a cave
Frodo is very weak, he could only walk up a peak
Merry is very wise and he knows if someone dies
Pippin has a knife, he could make anyone have a wife
Faramir he is so strong he could even break bong bong bongs
Éomer he is so fat that he lies down on his mat.

Ali Abdul Karim (9)
St Stephen's CE Primary School, Westminster

The Dragon

The dragon is yellow with glittering stripes.
When the people see him they wave sunny delight.
The dragon is scary but the people don't know.
The dragon comes out only for the snow.
The dragon likes to eat a pig,
But what they give him is a rotten twig.
The dragon has nasty savage teeth,
But don't forget he's made out of yellow beef.
His eyes are flashing red,
His belly looks like massive brown bread.
He acts like a baby, very, very cute,
He goes to sleep by the sound of a flute.
If you try to burn him down,
It will make an ugly sound.
Oh my! He's gone off very high,
I hope one day he will die.

Mohammed Aminul Hoque (10)
St Stephen's CE Primary School, Westminster

When I Go To School

When I go to school
Some people go so cool.

A girl got told off
Then Miss had to cough.

When Miss told us to listen
A boy got bitten by a kitten.

When Miss told us a rhyme
It took a bit of time.

A boy had the power
To eat the sweet sour.

Esraa Wadi (10)
St Stephen's CE Primary School, Westminster

Valentine

Not a red rose or a saint heart,
I give you a diamond,
A present meaning *love.*
It is a jewel that will shine on me, and
It promises the sigh of everlasting love
Like you and me will always be.

Here.
I will brighten up your day
Making the roses smell sweeter,
On a summer's day,
I will additionally bring
You happiness for I can do that.

I am trying to be truthful.
Not a cute card or a sweet kissogram.
I give you a taste of love that wills,
Also livening up your day.

Virginia Fuas (9)
St Stephen's CE Primary School, Westminster

In The Dark

He lies in bed all alone listening to the noises which surround him,
The wind whistles through a tiny hole in the cracked pane of glass.
He saw a shadow in the tree, he hid under the blanket.
Then he looked under the bed, and he saw three-headed dogs.
They were vicious, and then he woke up.

Brandon Black (10)
St Stephen's CE Primary School, Westminster

The Funny Clown

I once met a clown
Who walked upside down
He smelt a rose
And tickled his nose
He looked at his ted
And went to bed
He went to school
And he looked cool
He looked at his knife
And ran to his wife
He changed his clothes
And looked at his toes
He played with a ball
And it went over the wall
He had loads of bikes
These are all the things he likes
A train
A car
And going to the bar
He likes it to rain
But he's really insane.

Mariam Nahas (10)
St Stephen's CE Primary School, Westminster

Where Do I Come From?

It's in the west part of Africa,
It's a very small country,
It's usually sunny, and it's filled
With fresh fruit and palm trees.
It's a sandy and bright place throughout the year,
The languages we speak are Twi, Ashanti, Ga and others.
The colours of our flag are red,
Green, yellow and a black star.
Where do I come from?
The country is Ghana!

Emmalyn Ata-Gyamfi (10)
St Stephen's CE Primary School, Westminster

The Horrible Bear!

I went to the woods to get some fresh air,
Then I met a horrible bear!
Then I went on the ground to play dead,
Then I accidentally went to bed, (hee, hee!)
Then I sat on his old, creaky chair
Go you stupid bear!

Zahra Mohammed (10)
St Stephen's CE Primary School, Westminster

The Queen Of Wonderland

As I think about my future
I lie down and look at the sky
What will I be when I grow up I wonder?

Maybe I'll be a sailor one day!
Sail the mighty seas
Escape from the wavy sea water
Be captain and travel to all countries

Or maybe I'll be in the army!
Fight my enemies with guns
Blood flowing away on the ground
From people I killed violently

Should I be a teacher?
Shout at children when they're naughty?
Teach them literacy and art?
But what if they keep disrespecting me?

No! No! I'm going to be a doctor
Sit in my own room with a desk
Helping people with problems

My mum says I should be a hairdresser
Make different types of nice ones
People going out of the door with my fancy hairstyles
But what if they have greasy hair?

Dad says I should be a writer
Write things that nobody has ever written
Then I'll have no fun at all
All these answers can only be answered by
The Queen of Wonderland
For she is the one who knows all my wonders.

Mussammad Muntaha Syeda Uddin (10)
St Stephen's CE Primary School, Westminster

If I Was A Spider

If I was a spider
I would spin a web

Under a child's bed
And under a book

And under a chair
And under a teddy bear

And under the stairs
And under more chairs

And under the sink
Which is very pink,

Now's not the time
It's time for bed
Goodnight my friends

Go and rest your heads.

Toby Livsey (8)
The Falcons School for Boys

If I Was A 2p Coin

If I was a 2p coin
I would sit on a shelf.
If I was a 2p coin
I would spend myself.
If I was a 2p coin
I would go in a cash register.
If I was a 2p coin
I would be very small
Not very tall.

Jamie Young (8)
The Falcons School for Boys

If I Was The Lightning

If I was the lightning
I would flash
In the sky
Very very high.

If I was the lightning
I would strike
A tree and
Everyone would flee.

If I was the lightning
I would show
My light in
A very dark night.

Joshua Powell (8)
The Falcons School for Boys

If I Was A Shark

If I was a shark
I would snap, snap, snap
If I was a shark
I would swim with a snap
If I was a shark
I would eat, eat, eat
If I was a shark
I would eat your meat
If I was a shark
I would chase you away.

Aidan Ng (8)
The Falcons School for Boys

If I Was A Bird

If I was a bird
I'd fly in the sky

If I was a bird
I'd fly very high

If I was a bird
I'd spread each wing

If I was a bird
I'd sing sing sing

If I was a bird
I'd look at the land

If I was a bird
I'd walk on the sand.

Adam Stapleton (8)
The Falcons School for Boys

If I Was A Bird

If I was a bird
I would soar through the air.

If I was a bird
I would spread my wings and love the air.

If I was a bird
I would be cute and small.

If I was a bird
I would be happily enjoying my life.

If I was a bird
I would make a nest for my young.

Harrison Brewer (7)
The Falcons School for Boys

If I Was A Bird

If I was a bird,
My wings would spread,
I'd swoop over you
And glide by your head.

If I was a bird
I would fly up high
Among the clouds
Beyond the sky.

If I was a bird,
I would swoop down low,
Into the wilderness,
Where the rivers flow.

If I was a bird,
I would perch on a tree
And make a nest,
Where my chicks will be.

If I was a bird,
I'd curl up in a nest
And fold my wings,
To have a good rest.

Benedict Beltrami (7)
The Falcons School for Boys

Christmas

C hildren opening presents
H appy faces
R eindeer flying over houses
I ce on the roads
S nowflakes falling
T insel on Christmas trees
M essages in cards
A ngels in the sky
S anta coming down the chimney.

Archie Pearch (7)
The Falcons School for Boys

Autumn Days

Autumn is fun
Under trees
Eat a bun
Roll around in the autumn sun

Brown leaves
Crisp as carrot
Crackling below your feet

Autumn drizzle
Makes a puddle
People desperate
To get to their fires
With smoking chimneys.

Sam Jones (7)
The Falcons School for Boys

Weather Poem

Chilly drizzle raining mist though the trees
And feel the wind

It's a lot of fun to play in the autumn sun
And eat a bun.

Crackle crunch the leaves go
Also smells that go for miles.

Conkers, I'm collecting conkers
I'm trying hard to find the biggest and the best.

Autumn leaves on the ground
They blow like a spirit's around.

Charlie Farish (7)
The Falcons School for Boys

Autumn

Leaves rustling in the wind
Sticks crunching in the streets
Red, brown and yellow leaves in the trees.

Smoky chimneys on the houses
People warming up by fires
All snuggled up.

Oskar Goodwille (8)
The Falcons School for Boys

Autumn Fun

Lovely leaves autumn colour
Orange, brown, red, yellow.
Conkers falling, people calling.
Squirrels fighting over conkers.

Paul van der Merwe (8)
The Falcons School for Boys

Autumn Fun

Misty weather
Chilly feet
Very cold
But very weak

Conkers falling
From the trees
Children happy
As can be
What's that noise?
It's the sea

Feel the dry leaves
Crunching under your feet
Smell the smell
Fresh and sweet.

Rishi Patel-Warr (7)
The Falcons School for Boys

Autumn

Cold wind blowing in my face.
The rustling sound of
Leaves always in your mind.

All the conkers falling
Everybody calling for rain.

All the leaves on the ground
Turning brown, red, yellow and orange.

Squirrels jumping round and round
You and your front garden.

Oliver Johnson (7)
The Falcons School for Boys

Autumn

Hear the leaves
Crunching under your feet
With every step

Hear the wind
In the streets
Chilling you
From head to toe

Look up at the sky
The sky that keeps you dry
Autumn sun
Is bright and yellow

The leaves are
Brown, the weather
Is not, so
Don't complain

See the deer
And the squirrels eating
Conkers on the ground.

George Essex (7)
The Falcons School for Boys

Autumn Fun

The weather is cold and wet
Blowing in your face
Leaves on the floor
People cram around the fire
Leaves rustling around and about
In and out round and about
People rush around trying to keep warm.

Luke Olver (7)
The Falcons School for Boys

Christmas

C hildren opening presents
H appy people
R udolph visiting homes
I ce on the roads
S now everywhere
T insel on Christmas trees
M essages on cards
A ll the children are singing carols
S ummer is far away.

Rishi Anand (8)
The Falcons School for Boys

About Autumn

Autumn is great
Autumn is fun
Autumn is great for everyone

Noises are scary
Noises are loud
These are the sounds
From autumn ground

The weather is cold
The weather feels old
That is how the story is told

Autumn is cool
Autumn has trees
With yellow leaves

I feel cold
I need to be held
By my mum
This is fun.

Oliver Swan (8)
The Falcons School for Boys

Now The War Is Over

I looked outside,
People carrying knives who have fought for their lives.
It is the first time in a long time that no one was dying.
People only happy, laughing and crying.
In the field the first flower grew.
It was a poppy as we all knew.
I went and told my mother.
We went outside and hugged each other.
We gathered around it,
But then I saw my father.
I ran up to him.
We embraced each other.
Then I could live my life normally.

Molly McMorrow (9)
The Fox Primary School

Fairies

The world is old
But every spring
The world grows young
And the fairies sing.

Elisha Jelen (10)
The Fox Primary School

Angry

She's angry; she's a wild child,
She's angry; she's gone mad,
She's angry; can't we help this child?
She's angry, she's gone bad.
She's not allowed to watch TV or play computer games,
But if she doesn't get her way she goes into a rage.
She shouts and screams her head off if she doesn't get her way,
So we'll have to pull the plugs out and then see what she'll say!

Edie Gill Holder (10)
The Fox Primary School

The Phoenix

I dreamed of a phoenix
Who blew fire
And had wings,
That flapped like flames.

I dreamed of a phoenix,
With burning feathers.
His eyes lit up,
With a spark.

I dreamed of a phoenix,
Whose roar filled with passion.
His iron beak,
Blazed with strength.

I dreamed of a phoenix,
Who was never to be seen.
For its burning thought,
Turned my dream to ashes.

Ruby Lott-Lavigna (10)
The Fox Primary School

Snowflakes

Snowflakes fall like tears from your eyes
Snowflakes hit against your face like knives
Snowflakes stick together like trustworthy friends
Snowflakes wander till their journey ends.

Mo Langmuir (9)
The Fox Primary School

After The Party

After the party a sad feeling drifts around,
You think back to your favourite moments,
Like the popping of balloons
And eating the cake,
Or dancing to music.
The joy of having your friends all around you
Is the best thing,
You want to capture the moment.
But you can't - what a nightmare!
Soon the feeling's gone, it flickers and fades,
Like the flame on a birthday candle.
And won't return for another year.
After the party the air feels bittersweet,
As sour as lemon juice,
As empty as a popped balloon,
But somewhere deep down is a warm glow,
And even though you're upset you know it's been worthwhile.
Maybe next year you'll be ready for the nightmare after the party.

Tatiana Zoe Barnes (9)
The Fox Primary School

Sir Francis Drake

Sir Francis Drake was a sailor, sailor, sailor
Who travelled the seven seas
And went through some cold degrees
He travelled for years and heard lots of cheers
And he said he was glad to be he.

He had some tears and he had some cheers
The years went slow and fast
And he was sure to remember the past
The sea was rough but he was tough
Nothing was a task for him.

Lauren Fisher (9)
West Acton Primary School

Springtime

S pring has come
P etals peeping, chicks cheeping
R abbits running, colours coming
I n the field. Here is the sun
N ow that wet winter is done
G lorious spring has come.

Kayli Homer (10)
West Acton Primary School

The Monster Under My Bed

The monster is bigger than a giant ogre
His teeth are gigantic and so is his head
The monster is a massive beast and he is sneaking
The monster comes sneaking, sneaking and sneaking
Creeping out from under my bed.

Ethan Harry Hart-Badger (9)
West Acton Primary School

The Man Invasion

There once was an alien who believed in mankind
But it turned out the alien didn't have a mind
One day the alien was abducted by man
While he was on Earth he got a weird tan
But the alien had missed his home so the alien came
Flying, flying, flying up to his home planet Mars.

Ameenah Aumeed (9)
West Acton Primary School

Spooky

The ghost was scary like a monster's claws.
The graveyard was creepy like a creaky old door.
The monster claws were very sharp like a shark
And the bats came flying and flying.
The bats came flying over the graveyard in the dark.

Amanda Lee (10)
West Acton Primary School

The Mad Family

The mad family was a monster's breath
The house was a prison of deadly death
And the family kept on shouting -
Shouting - shouting
The family kept on shouting for all the years to come

About two mad years later
The mad son became a waiter
And all the food kept dropping -
Dropping - dropping
And all the food kept dropping onto the customers' heads

The normal neighbours were complaining
Because the electricity kept failing
Because the family kept breaking -
Breaking - breaking
Because the family kept breaking the wires around the house

As you can see the family is *very* mad
Though often they get very sad
And I cannot really tell you -
Tell you - tell you
I cannot really tell you more madness as there's far too much to add.

Hannah Roiter (10)
West Acton Primary School

The Ugly Alien

The alien was ugly and dumb
The space was shaped like a drum
The alien among the stars
And the alien came flying, flying, flying
The alien came flying, up from Mars.

The alien's silly cat
Was shaped like a bat
That cat went on the alien's back
And the alien came running, running, running
The alien came running, into the house pack.

The alien went back
And he had his sack,
He said, 'This place is too big.'
And the alien went flying, flying, flying
The alien went flying, back to his space pig.

Mona Roozfarakh (9)
West Acton Primary School

The Big-Headed Alien

The sky was dark blue swaying sea
The alien's head was bigger than you and me
And the alien came glowing,
Glowing, glowing.
The alien came flying, flying,
The alien came
Flying down to Earth.

His head was like a flying saucer
His feet were coarse but his elbows were coarser.
The freaky thing was he could remember his own birth
And his tummy looked like a smiling Smurf.

Laura Alicia Hall-Williams (9)
West Acton Primary School